BRITISH RAILWAYS STEAMING ON THE EX-LNER LINES

Volume One

Compiled by

PETER HANDS & COLIN RICHARDS

DEFIANT PUBLICATIONS
190 Yoxall Road
Shirley, Solihull
West Midlands

Printed in the United Kingdom by Netherwood Dalton & Co. Ltd., Huddersfield, England.

CURRENT STEAM PHOTOGRAPH ALBUMS AVAILABLE
FROM DEFIANT PUBLICATIONS

VOLUME 3
A4 size - Hardback. 100 pages
- 182 b/w photographs.
£7.95 + 75p postage.
ISBN 0 946857 02 4.

VOLUME 4
A4 size - Hardback. 100 pages
- 182 b/w photographs.
£7.95 + 75p postage.
ISBN 0 946857 04 0.

VOLUME 5
A4 size - Hardback. 100 pages
- 180 b/w photographs.
£7.95 + 75p postage.
ISBN 0 946857 06 7.

VOLUME 6
A4 size - Hardback. 100 pages
- 182 b/w photographs.
£8.45 + 75p postage.
ISBN 0 946857 08 3.

VOLUME 7
A4 size - Hardback. 100 pages
- 182 b/w photographs.
£8.45 + 75p postage.
ISBN 0 946857 10 5.

VOLUME 8
A4 size - Hardback. 100 pages
- 181 b/w photographs.
£8.95 + 75p postage.
ISBN 0 946857 14 8.

VOLUME 9
A4 size - Hardback. 100 pages
- 182 b/w photographs.
£9.95 + 75p postage.
ISBN 0 946857 18 0.

VOLUME 10
IN
PREPARATION
NOVEMBER 1988

VOLUME 1
A4 size - Hardback. 100 pages
-180 b/w photographs.
£8.95 + 75p postage.
ISBN 0 946857 12 1.

VOLUME 2
A4 size - Hardback. 100 pages
-180 b/w photographs.
£8.95 + 75p postage.
ISBN 0 946857 13 X.

VOLUME 3
A4 size - Hardback. 100 pages
- 180 b/w photographs.
£9.95 + 75p postage.
ISBN 0 946857 16 4.

VOLUME 4
A4 size - Hardback. 100 pages
- 180 b/w photographs
£9.95 + 75p postage.
ISBN 0 946857 17 2.

CURRENT STEAM PHOTOGRAPH ALBUMS AVAILABLE
FROM DEFIANT PUBLICATIONS

VOLUME 5
IN
PREPARATION
MARCH 1989

VOLUME 6
IN
PREPARATION
MARCH 1989

VOLUME 7

VOLUME 8

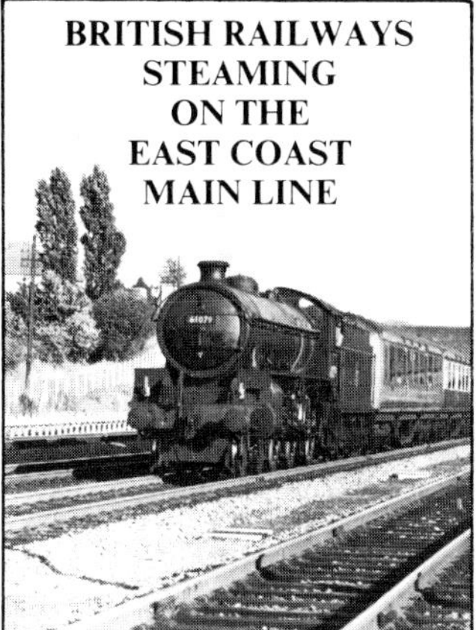

A4 size - Hardback. 100 pages
- 183 b/w photographs.
£8.95 + 75p postage.
ISBN 0 946857 07 5.
(Reprinted July 1988)

VOLUME 1
A4 size - Hardback. 100 pages
- 187 b/w photographs.
£9.95 + 75p postage.
ISBN 0 946857 19 9.

VOLUME 1
A4 size - Hardback. 100 pages
- 188 b/w photographs.
£8.45 + 75p postage.
ISBN 0 946857 09 1.

VOLUME 2
IN
PREPARATION
NOVEMBER 1988

VOLUME 1
A4 size - Hardback. 100 pages
- 188 b/w photographs.
£7.95 + 75p postage.
ISBN 0 946857 03 2.

VOLUME 2
A4 size - Hardback. 100 pages
- 181 b/w photographs.
£8.45 + 75p postage.
ISBN 0 946857 11 3.

VOLUME 1
A4 size - Hardback. 100 pages
- 184 b/w photographs.
£7.95 + 75p postage.
ISBN 0 946857 05 9.

VOLUME 2
A4 size - Hardback. 100 pages
- 181 b/w photographs.
£8.95 + 75p postage.
ISBN 0 946857 15 6.

OTHER TITLES AVAILABLE FROM DEFIANT PUBLICATIONS

PRICES VARY FROM £1 to £3.80 INCLUDING POSTAGE

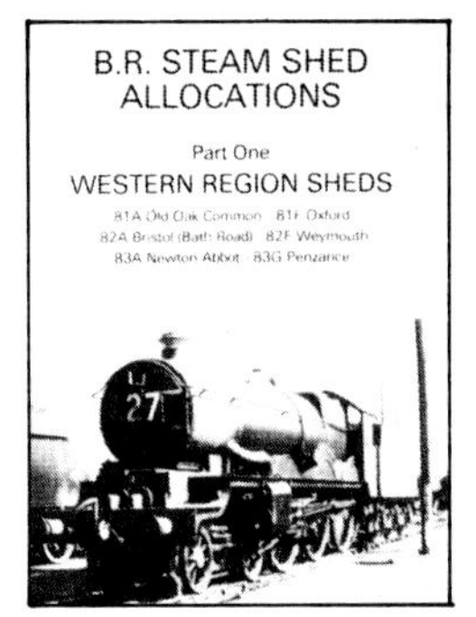

WHAT HAPPENED TO STEAM

This series of booklets, 50 in all, is designed to inform the reader of the allocations, re-allocations and dates of withdrawal of steam locomotives during their last years of service. From 1957 onwards and finally where the locomotives concerned were stored and subsequently scrapped.

BR STEAM SHED ALLOCATIONS

This series lists all individual steam locomotives based at the different parent depots of B.R. from January 1957 until each depot either closed to steam or closed completely. All regions have been completed with the exception of the London Midland which will be dealt with during 1987.

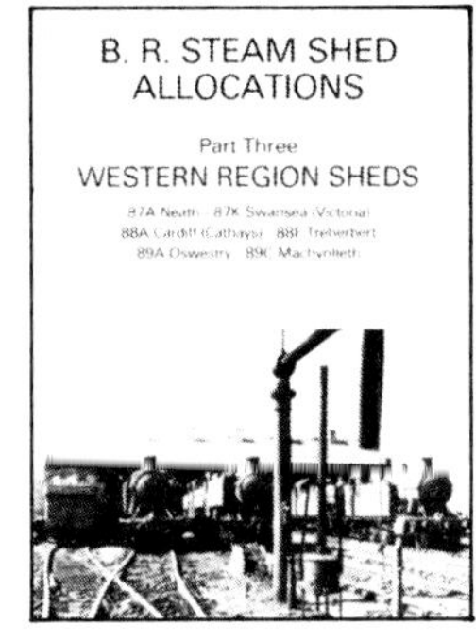

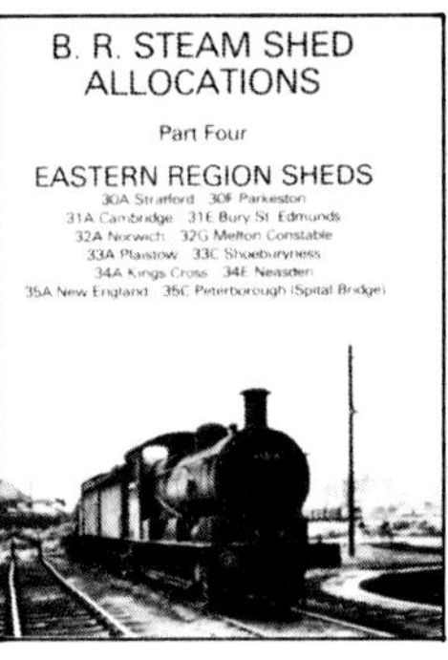

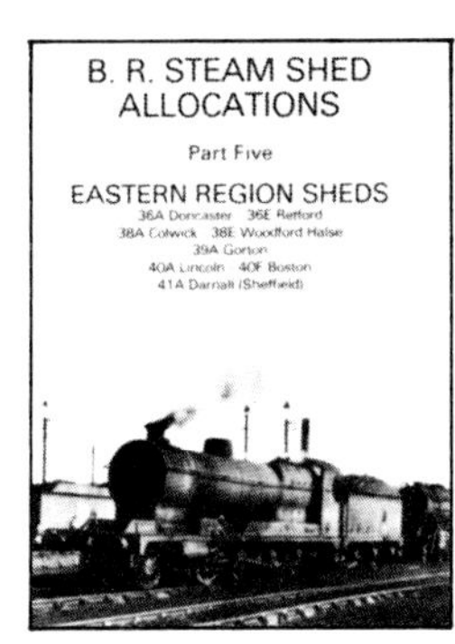

CHASING STEAM ON SHED

PETER HANDS

BARBRYN PRESS £5.95 + 50p POSTAGE

ISBN 0 906160 030

This is an account of a locospotters life during the years of 1956-1968. In 1956 when there were 18 000 or so steam locomotives on B.R. it was every locospotters ambition to set eyes on as many locomotives as possible, especially before they were withdrawn.

Every trainspotter will remember "shed bashing" trips, some official, mostly unofficial, the challenge they represented and the feeling of delight of having achieved of what was regarded in some cases as the impossible. All these are relived with an almost uncanny accurateness.

We also plot through the various exploits of other railway trips of which there are many positively hilarious accounts and these are backed up most commendably by a series of cartoon illustrations which often capture the mood and atmosphere of those days so perfectly.

Depending on your age, this book will either bring back lots of memories, make you realise what you missed or if you were too young to participate will let you realise what good days they were.

....

Lineside Camera Series by G. W. Sharpe.

	8″ × 8″ Approx
East Coast Pacifics	48 Pages £1.95 + 30p postage.
Yorkshire Steam	48 Pages £1.95 + 30p postage.
Pennine Steam	48 Pages £1.95 + 30p postage.
BR Standard Steam	36 Pages £2.25 + 30p postage.
Diesels in the Sixties	36 Pages £2.25 + 30p postage.

ACKNOWLEDGEMENTS

Grateful thanks are extended to the following contributors of photographs not only for their use in this book but for their kind patience and long term loan of negatives/photographs whilst this book was being compiled.

D. ALEXANDER MORECAMBE	G. D. APPLEYARD MIDDLESBROUGH
H. H. BLEADS BIRMINGHAM	B. W. L. BROOKSBANK LONDON
N. L. BROWNE ALDERSHOT	L. BROWNHILL BRIERLEY HILL
R. S. CARPENTER BIRMINGHAM	J. K. CARTER MILLHOLME
K. FOSTER SCARBOROUGH	A. N. H. GLOVER BIRMINGHAM
J. D. GOMERSALL SHEFFIELD	PETER HAY HOVE
J. HEAD TENTERDEN	R. W. HINTON GLOUCESTER
F. HORNBY NORTH CHEAM	A. C. INGRAM WISBECH
H. N. JAMES IPSWICH	D. K. JONES MOUNTAIN ASH
M. JOYCE HITCHIN	R. LEITCH SAWSTON
R. PICTON WOLVERHAMPTON	W. POTTER BISHOPS CLEEVE
N. E. PREEDY HUCCLECOTE	P. A. ROWLINGS ALCONBURY
K. L. SEAL ANDOVERSFORD	G. W. SHARPE BARNSLEY
C. P. STACEY STONY STRATFORD	M. S. STOKES MARPLE
JOHN STONES TUNBRIDGE WELLS	G. WOOD BIRMINGHAM

Front Cover – Dense clouds of black smoke erupts from the double chimney of Peppercorn A1 Class 4-6-2 No 60124 *Kenilworth* (52A Gateshead) as it blasts out of Peterborough (North) station with a Kings Cross to Newcastle express in 1958. Constructed at Doncaster by BR in 1949, *Kenilworth* was only nine years old when this picture was taken. (A. C. Ingram)

ISBN 0 946857 19 9   ©P. B. HANDS/C. RICHARDS 1988
FIRST PUBLISHED 1988

INTRODUCTION

BRITISH RAILWAYS STEAMING ON THE EX-LNER LINES – Volume One, is the second book to concentrate on the now British Railways tracks and locomotives once owned or influenced by this once great railway company. The authors hope the reader will enjoy the diverse variety of locomotives and locations within the pages of this album.

The 'BR Steaming' books are designed to give the ordinary, everyday steam photographic enthusiast of the 1950's and 1960's a chance to participate in and give pleasure to others whilst recapturing the twilight days of steam.

Apart from the 1950's and 1960's series, individual regional albums, like this one, will be produced from time to time. Wherever possible, no famous names will be found nor will photographs which have been published before be used. Nevertheless, the content and quality of the majority of photographs selected will be second to none.

The layout of **BRITISH RAILWAYS STEAMING ON THE EX-LNER LINES** – Volume One differs from **BRITISH RAILWAYS STEAMING ON THE EAST COAST MAIN LINE** in as much that it does not concentrate on a single route. This album is divided into three chapters covering the Eastern, North Eastern and Scottish Regions of British Railways from 1948-67, by which time allocated steam had finished on all three regions. Unless otherwise stated all locomotives are of LNER origin.

The purists may argue that not all of the locations and locomotives included in this album are of pure LNER origin. The authors have included some photographs of areas taken over by the BR Regions and of locomotives constructed after nationalisation in 1948 but allocated to the same. The authors have also attempted to vary the locations as much as possible but some areas of greater interest e.g. Doncaster, Edinburgh and York etc., have been given more coverage than others.

The majority of the photographs used in this album have been contributed by readers of Peter Hands series of booklets entitled "What Happened to Steam' & "BR Steam Shed Allocations" and from readers of the earlier "BR Steaming Through the Sixties" albums. In normal circumstances these may have been hidden from the public eye forever.

The continuation of the "BR Steaming" series etc., depends upon you the reader. If you feel you have suitable material of BR steam locomotives between 1948-1968 and wish to contribute them towards this series and other future publications please contact either:

<table>
<tr><td>Peter Hands,
190 Yoxall Road,
Shirley, Solihull,
West Midlands B90 3RN</td><td>OR</td><td>Colin Richards,
28 Kendrick Close,
Damson Parkway, Solihull,
West Midlands B92 0QD</td></tr>
</table>

CONTENTS

EASTERN REGION

	PAGES
NAMEPLATES	5
Annesley	15
Barnsley	11
Barnwell Junction	16
Cambridge	6/18
Clacton	32
Colchester	14
Colwich	26
Crowle	36
Darnall (Sheffield)	9
Doncaster	13/35/37
Ely	28
Enfield	19
Epping	9
Finsbury Park	17
Frodingham	33
Grantham	30
Hatfield	19
Ipswich	32
Kings Cross	12/27/31
Kings Lynn	35
Langwith Junction	7
Lincoln	16
Louth	25
Lowestoft	34
March	8/36
Marks Tey	20/22
Mildenhall	24
Neasden	12
New England	14/18
Norwich	17
Peterborough	21/29/33/37 & Front Cover
Potters Bar	34
Retford	13/28
Sheffield	23
Shoeburyness	21
Southend	20
Spital Bridge	23/26
Stamford Junction	27
Staveley	10
Stratford	15/22/24/31
Thorpe-le-Soken	25
Tilbury	29
Werrington	8
West Ham	30
Whittlesea	10
Witham	7
Yarmouth	11

NORTH EASTERN REGION

	PAGES
Ardsley	41
Arthington Junction	67
Darlington	43/48/59/63
Durham	Rear Cover Top
Easington	48
Farnley Junction	56/60
Gateshead	62
Goole	39/54
Harton	62
Headingley	66
Huddersfield	55
Hull	51/54
Leeds	49/56/58/63/65
Low Moor	52/66
Monkton Moor	61
Newcastle	41/42/46/64
Newsham	53/59
Normanton	38/50
Percy Main	39/49
Pilmoor	58
Ripon	51/57
Royston	52
Scarborough	55
South Pelaw	42
Sowerby Bridge	50
Stockton	43/47/64
Thirsk	45
Thornaby	45/61
Tyne Dock	44
West Hartlepool	40/46/53/57
York	40/44/47/60/65/67

SCOTTISH REGION

	PAGES
Aberdeen	74/76
Aberlour	69
Arbroath	96
Bathgate	83
Carnoustie	80
Coatbridge	82
Craigellachie	87
Craigendoran	80
Cowlairs	79/88
Dundee	68/89
Dunfermline	70/75/78/91/94
Eastfield (Glasgow)	84/91
Edinburgh	77/83/86/88/89/90/93
Elgin	90
Fort William	81
Haymarket	74/94
Inverbervie	73
Keith	71/92
Kipps	77/85/96
Kittybrewster	72/81/86/92
Parkhead	69/75/82
Partick Hill Junction	84
Seafield	78
South Leith	71
St. Margarets (Edinburgh)	72/76/95 & Rear Cover Bottom
Thornton Junction	70/73/79/85/87/93
West Ferry	95

NAMEPLATES – Some example nameplates of L.N.E.R. locomotives.

1) A4 Class 4-6-2 No 60034 *Lord Faringdon*. (R. Picton)

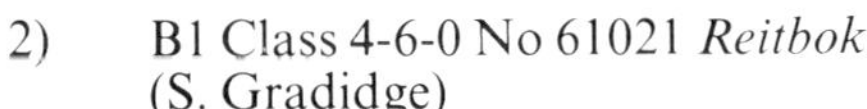

2) B1 Class 4-6-0 No 61021 *Reitbok*. (S. Gradidge)

3) B17 Class 4-6-0 No 61657 *Doncaster Rovers*. (N. L. Browne)

4) D11 Class 4-4-0 No 62666 *Zeebrugge* (N. L. Browne)

5) D49 Class 4-4-0 No 62761 *The Derwent*. (Peter Hay)

CHAPTER ONE – EASTERN REGION

6)   Amidst a swirl of leaking steam, Thompson B1 Class 4-6-0 No 61360, from 30E Colchester, departs from Cambridge on a gloomy day in 1958 with an express bound for Liverpool Street, consisting in the main of Gresley coaches. 61360 was re-allocated to 31A Cambridge in April 1959 and in November of the same year was drafted to 36A Doncaster where it remained in service until withdrawn in April 1966, the same month as steam ceased to exist on the Eastern Region. (A. C. Ingram)

7)   The branch train from Maldon (East) was an all GER affair on 21st May 1956, as it arrived at Witham, junction for the main line and the branch to Braintree. The engine with ex. GER carriages is ex. GER F5 Class 2-4-2T No 67189. The Maldon branch and its associated stations at Langford & Ulting and Wickham Bishops closed in 1964, but we can still go by train to Braintree. (Peter Hay)

8)   Pure Great Central is captured by the camera as late as 21st June 1964. At rest in the shed yard of the former GC shed at 41J Langwith Junction is ex. GC Robinson 'ROD' O4/3 Class 2-8-0 No 63861, a native of the depot. 63861 survived until February 1965 but the shed lingered on until total closure twelve months later. Coded 40E for many years, Langwith Junction was used to supply locomotives mostly for freight traffic. (N. E. Preedy)

9)   Brilliant Spring sunshine reflects off the clean lines of ex. GER J17 Class 0-6-0 No 65562 as it awaits its next duty in the yard of its home shed at 31B March on 11th April 1954. Designed by Holden and introduced into service in 1901, these locomotives were employed on local passenger and light freight duties. 65562 ended its days at 31A Cambridge being withdrawn in August 1958. (G. Wood)

10)   The sign in the left of this picture once pointed to the familiar but now long gone water troughs which were to be found on the majority of main lines on British Railways with the exception of the Southern Region. A1 Class 4-6-2 No 60129 *Guy Mannering* (52A Gateshead) is photographed near to Werrington troughs, between Peterborough and Tallington, in 1958 at the head of a Kings Cross to Newcastle express. (A. C. Ingram)

11)   The lineside cabling is standard London Transport equipment in this picture, so it cannot be some remote ex. GER branch line. In fact the two coach train, hauled by ex. GER F5 Class 2-4-2T No 67193 is nearing Epping, where, on 1st April 1956 the Central Line tube trains ended their journeys into Essex. Passengers who wished to go further, transferred to a real train like this one, for the last lap to Ongar. (Peter Hay)

12)   The large straight running shed at 41A Darnall (Sheffield) is overlooked by the massive concrete coaling plant on 27th January 1962. A rather fed-up looking coloured member of the shed staff poses for the camera whilst behind him simmers K3 Class 2-6-0 No 61847 (50B Hull – Dairycoates) and B1 Class 4-6-0 No 61312, a local inhabitant of Darnall. (P. A. Rowlings)

13) The former Midland Railway shed at 18D Staveley (Barrow Hill), became Eastern Region property in February 1958, being re-coded 41E. For many years the depot had supplied shunting engines to the nearby steelworks and on 23rd August 1963 ex. MR Class 1F 0-6-0T No. 41804 is photographed on such a duty. In the foreground, travelling too fast for the camera shutter, is a small boy showing a smart turn of speed on his bicycle. (B. W. L. Brooksbank)

14) The chimneys of Whittlesea brickworks make an unusual background for the 12.37 pm, four coach express passenger from Peterborough (North) to Cambridge as it romps along, in a haze of black smoke, on the level fenland track behind D16/3 Class 4-4-0 No 62548 on 3rd April 1953. 62548, depot unknown on this date, managed to survive in service until September 1957, being withdrawn from 31B March. (Peter Hay)

15)   Maximum occupation at 32D Yarmouth South Town shed in 1957. The once stream-lined B17 Class 4-6-0 No 61659 *East Anglian* is at rest in front of the roof-less depot building. The roof was rebuilt in late 1958/early 1959, an apparent waste of time and money as the shed closed completely in November 1959. *East Anglian*, a local engine, moved on to 32C Lowestoft in December 1958. (R. S. Carpenter)

16)   When full of locomotives, the yard and shed at 36D Barnsley became rather congested as can be seen by the row of engines parked under the bridge near to the depot. One of the locally based ex. GCR J11 Class 0-6-0 No 64452 is out of steam on 7th April 1957. Re-coded 41G in February 1958, Barnsley which closed in January 1960 was demolished the same year. (F. Hornby)

17) Its cylinders charged with steam, Thompson B1 Class 4-6-0 No 61033 *Dibatag* (home depot unknown) makes a spirited departure from Kings Cross and heads for Cambridge with an express on 19th May 1956. *Dibatag* was one of fifty-nine members of the class which were named, many at random. The majority were named after species of antelope and most of the remaining ones after the upper crust of the railway hierarchy. (N. L. Browne)

18) L3 Class 2-6-4T No 69061 at 34E Neasden, the GCR London shed, was working out its mileage before withdrawal when photographed on 25th June 1952. These massive engines never realised their true potential because, despite their 97½ tons weight, they lacked brake power. They could pull large loads but sometimes found it difficult to stop them when going downhill. 69061 was taken out of service in February 1953. (Peter Hay)

19) Minus tender, left-hand cylinder and with various metal odds and ends piled above the front bufferbeam, the end looks nigh for A3 Class 4-6-2 No 60062 *Minoru,* at Doncaster Works on 27th January 1962. However there was still life ahead for *Minoru,* from 34E New England, as it was at 'The Plant' for a 'P & V Exam' as chalked on the cab and cylinder casing. (P. A. Rowlings)

20) Ex. Great Central Railway 'Large Director' D11 Class 4-4-0 No 62666 *Zeebrugge,* in quite deplorable external condition, with a rake of typical 'blood & custard' stock of the day, pauses at Retford with a local Sheffield (Victoria) to Lincoln stopping train on 28th May 1955. Presumably based at 40A Lincoln, *Zeebrugge* spent the last few years of its working life based at 41A Darnall (Sheffield) being condemned from there in December 1960. (J. D. Gomersall)

21)   The clean exhaust from Peppercorn A1 Class 4-6-2 No 60123 *H. A. Ivatt* is captured brilliantly by the camera in 1959. *H. A. Ivatt* a 56C Copley Hill locomotive is on the down *Harrogate Sunday Pullman* near to New England depot at Peterborough. Based at Copley Hill from September 1957 to March 1962, *H. A. Ivatt* was one of the first of the class to be condemned, in October 1962 from 56B Ardsley. (A. C. Ingram)

22)   With its tender filled to the brim with coal, 31B March based ex. GER J20 Class 0-6-0 No 64699 simmers gently in bright sunshine as it awaits its next turn of duty in a siding at 30E Colchester on 24th May 1958. 64699 remained in revenue earning service at March depot until withdrawn in September 1962. Stored at March for over a year it was finally cut up at Doncaster Works in September 1963. (F. Hornby)

23)   A begrimed ex. GNR J50/1 Class 0-6-0T No 68896 is noted in light steam in the yard of its home shed at 38B Annesley on 30th September 1956. 68896 is sporting an express headcode and a tarpaulin is strung across the cab to help keep the elements at bay. Annesley passed to LMR control in February 1958 being coded 16D. It again changed codes in September 1963 to 16B and closed early in January 1966. (A. N. H. Glover)

24)   Warm sunshine and a busy location was just the ticket for photographers and spotters alike in steam days. L1 Class 2-6-4T No 67778, from the nearby depot, shunts vans under the wires at Stratford on 7th June 1959. Transferred to Stratford from Neasden in January 1959, 67778 returned to Neasden in August 1960. In December 1960 it found itself at 34E New England where it finally ended its days in May 1962. (N. L. Browne)

25)   In 1884 a branch was opened from the Cambridge – Ely line to Fordham on the Ely – Newmarket line. This signalbox
was provided at Barnwell Junction, a station which had platforms only on the branch. Passing on an Ely to
Cambridge train on 2nd April 1956 is D16 Class 4-4-0 No 62558 which has retained its original outside framing.
Notice that the signalman has prematurely restored his home signal!!! (Peter Hay)

26)   One of the huge ex. GCR A5/1 Class 4-6-2 Tanks No 69815, from 40E Langwith Junction, is out of steam in the yard
at 40A Lincoln on a misty 19th September 1954. Constructed at Gorton Works in June 1917, 69815 had a working life
of forty years before being taken out of service from 39A Gorton in July 1957. It was cut up at Darlington Works the
same month. (F. Hornby)

27)   Two generations of express power on shed at 32A Norwich on 5th April 1956. In the foreground is ex. GER B12 Class
       4-6-0 No 61540, although re-boilered by the LNER, representing the pre-Grouping era, whilst in the background BR
       Britannia Class 4-6-2 No 70040 *Clive of India*. Peeping out of the shed building is K3 Class 2-6-0 No 61970. (Peter Hay)

28)   Although some twenty-eight years old, A3 Class 4-6-2 No 60039 *Sandwich* lends majesty to the scene as it rumbles over
       an iron bridge at Finsbury Park, two short miles or so from Kings Cross, with an unidentified express on 21st April
       1962. *Sandwich*, allocated to 34A Kings Cross had been equipped with a double chimney in July 1959 and fitted with
       German style smoke deflectors in June 1961. (R. Leitch)

29)   At Cambridge the Mildenhall branch train in July 1952 was still completely GER. The Class J15 0-6-0 No 65474 was built in 1913, one of the last of its type, while the GER carriages with their stubby door handles and extra long handrails are of about the same age, though downgraded from the main line duties for which they were constructed. (Peter Hay)

30)   The nearest large passenger engine shed to Kings Cross on the East Coast Main Line was at New England, to the north of Peterborough station. Ready for its next duty and in good external condition on 7th April 1956 is A2/2 Class 4-6-2 No 60505 *Thane of Fife,* seen here by the coaling plant. *Thane of Fife,* fitted with small smoke deflectors, was a local engine of the then coded 35A shed and ended its life there in November 1959. (A. N. H. Glover)

31) One of the sub-sheds which came under the control of 30A Stratford was at Enfield Town, a small straight structure situated next to the station platform. Standing in front of the shed on 20th September 1958 are a duet of GER N7 Class 0-6-2 Tanks Nos 69657 and 69668. In the station is sister engine No 69665 with the 2.19 pm to Liverpool Street. All three engines were based at Stratford. Enfield shed closed in November 1960. (F. Hornby)

32) A grubby looking L1 Class 2-6-4T No 67793, from 34A Kings Cross, leaves a trail of murky exhaust behind it as it approaches Hatfield station with a Hitchin to Kings Cross local passenger train on 20th September 1958. 67793 was made redundant from 34A Kings Cross in May 1962 and sent to 40E Colwick where it survived for only a few months before being condemned in September of the same year. (F. Hornby)

33) The leading carriage of this three coach train from Cambridge to Colchester is ex. GER, quite distinct from the Gresley style which the LNER produced. Ex. GER 'Claud Hamilton' D16/3 Class 4-4-0 No 62610 has left the single Colne Valley line for main line double track at Marks Tey on the last lap into Colchester on 21st May 1956. (Peter Hay)

34) From the end of the Second World War in 1945, the B12 Class 4-6-0's played a major part in working the Liverpool Street – Southend (Victoria) services and on Sunday 11th March 1956 No 61516 was on shed at 30D Southend, in company with other members of the class and a B17 Class 4- 6-0. Somebody has taken the trouble to clean its lining and paint the smokebox hinges. (Peter Hay)

35)   In 1949 the former LMR sheds on the London, Tilbury & Southend Railway at Plaistow, Shoeburyness and Tilbury
were transferred to the Eastern Region. By 1958 all of the Stanier 3 cylinder Class 4 2-6-4 Tanks were based at 33C
Shoeburyness. Photographed in the shed yard on 13th April 1958 is No 42501. Nos 42500-36 were withdrawn by June
1962. (A. N. H. Glover)

36)   White smoke fills the roof space at Peterborough (North) as Gresley A4 Class 4-6-2 No 60003 *Andrew K. McCosh*
(34A Kings Cross) drifts into the station at the head of an unknown express on 24th February 1962. Constructed at
Doncaster Works in 1937, *Andrew K. McCosh* was one of the first five members of the class to be withdrawn from
service, during December 1962, the others being Nos 60014/28/30/33 all based at Kings Cross. (R. Leitch)

37)	Tank engine power in the yard at 30A Stratford shed on 7th June 1959. From right to left are J68 Class 0-6-0T No 68644, J69 Class 0-6- 0T No 68549 and N7 Class 0-6-2T No 69686. All three locomotives were native to Stratford and were withdrawn from service November 1960, February 1962 and September 1961 respectively. (F. Hornby)

38)	A train from Cambridge to Colchester crosses the lofty viaduct over the Colne Valley near Marks Tey on 21st May 1956. The engine, travelling backwards, with a tender-cab is ex. GER J15 Class 0-6-0 No 65438 and the train comprises of two non-corridor carriages with an ex. GER corridor between them. (Peter Hay)

39)   Rows of terraced houses and a large factory provide a backdrop to this photograph of a WD Austerity Class 8F 2-8-0 No 90709 as it clanks along at the head of a lengthy mineral train in Sheffield in 1958. In stark contrast to todays railway scene in Sheffield, after all the years of rationalisation, in the 1950's the 'City of Steel' was a mass of activity and a host of never ending lines. (G. W. Sharpe)

40)   Peterborough possessed two steam sheds, one of Great Northern Railway origin, at New England and the other at Spital Bridge was once owned by the Midland Railway and later by the London Midland Region. During 1950 it became the property of the Eastern Region. LMS Ivatt Class 2-6-0 No 46466, a visitor from 31A Cambridge, takes refreshment in the yard in September 1958. (A. C. Ingram)

41) 1959 was the last real year of service for the 'Sandringham' B2 & B17 Classes of 4-6-0's on the Eastern Region, although a few lingered on into 1960 being employed on menial duties. B17 No 61613 *Woodbastwick Hall* (31A Cambridge) looks in fine fettle as it blackens the skyline passing under the wires at Stratford on 7th June 1959 with a Cambridge express. December of this same year saw the end of this locomotive. (N. L. Browne)

42) The Cambridge – Mildenhall service was one of the last regularly worked by engines of the 2-4-0 wheel arrangement in Britain. Despite having a tender cab, ex. GER E4 Class 2-4-0 No 62796 in atrocious condition, was being turned after arrival at Mildenhall on 2nd April 1956, to be the right way round for the return to Cambridge. The two coach branch train is on the left, alongside the platform. (Peter Hay)

43) A modern looking building overlooks the shabby two road shed at 40C Louth on 19th September 1954. Parker M.S. & L. N5 Class 0-6-2T No 69309, a resident of this shed and in a filthy condition is carrying an express headcode whilst out of steam in the small yard. Louth shed closed completely in December 1956. At one time it had been owned by the Great Northern Railway. (F. Hornby)

44) The 10.36 am Liverpool Street to Clacton Interval Service restarts from Thorpe-le-Soken Junction where it has shed the three coaches for Frinton and Walton. They continued their journey behind a Class J15 0-6-0, while BR *Britannia* Class 4-6-2 No 70005 *John Milton* (30A Stratford) worked the main train through to Clacton. At the opposite platform the 12 noon Interval train to Liverpool Street is just leaving on 17th June 1958. (Peter Hay)

45)   The interior of 31F Spital Bridge (Peterborough) in June 1959. From left to right are ex. LMS Class 4F 0-6-0 No
        44476, an unidentified ex. GER D16 Class 4-4-0, ex. LMS Class 0-6-0 No 43957 and sister engine No 44509 all based
        at Spital Bridge. The allocation at this shed was very small compared to its counterpart at New England and it closed
        in February 1960. (H. H. Bleads)

46)   On the outskirts of the City of Nottingham was the massive freight orientated depot which was situated at Colwick.
        Many classes of locomotives were housed here and on 30th September 1956 one of its fleet of B1 Class 4-6-0's No
        61201 is being prepared for the road. At this stage in time the code for the depot was 38A which was to change in
        February 1958 to 40E. (A. N. H. Glover)

47)   The transfer goods from Essendine on the East Coast Main Line arrives at Stamford Junction early one morning in
April 1956. The lines on the right lead to Peterborough, on the LMR line from Leicester. Like the passenger services
the Essendine goods is worked by a C12 Class 4- 4-2T, in this case No 67394. (Peter Hay)

48)   Bright afternoon sunshine highlights the imminent departure of A4 Class 4-6-2 No 60015 *Quicksilver* (34A Kings
Cross) from Kings Cross at the head of the 3.10 pm express to Newcastle on 18th August 1959. *Quicksilver* remained
at Kings Cross shed until withdrawn from service in April 1963. Stored at Doncaster Works she was to be reduced to a
pile of scrap in June 1963 at her birthplace. (M. Joyce)

49)   A very typical East Anglian sight in the 1950's: a three coach local train ambling along in the charge of a begrimed ex. GER 'Claud Hamilton' D16 Class 4-4-0. This is No 62564, from 32A Norwich, one of a number that retained the decorative valances over the coupling rods, arriving at Ely on 3rd April 1956. The steaming days of 62564 were brought to an end in March 1958. (Peter Hay)

50)   The yard at 36E Retford G. N. plays host to a locally based engine B1 Class 4-6-0 No 61212 on 21st June 1964, just five months prior to withdrawal. 61212 was to fall prey, like legions of other locomotives, to the cutters torch at Drapers of Hull, in this case in April 1965. Retford G. N. closed its doors forever in June 1965. (N. E. Preedy)

51)	Amidst a mass of tracks at Peterborough North Sidings on a summer's day in 1958, the crew of Thompson 1946 built A2/3 Class 4-6-2 No 60500 *Edward Thompson* (34E New England) pass the time of day as they wait for a northbound express which they will take over. *Edward Thompson* in squalid external condition, is equipped with an ugly rimless double chimney and has a partially scorched smokebox. (A. C. Ingram)

52)	The 0-6-2 Tanks were the London, Tilbury & Southend Railway's equivalent of the common 0-6-0 goods engine, easy gradients and short runs making a tender unnecessary either for coal, water or braking. Class 3F No 41991 is bringing a train of oil tanks past Tilbury (West) signalbox on 13th April 1953. (Peter Hay)

53)   The Richmond – North Woolwich electrics use these tracks now, but in July 1956 all trains were steam worked like this short goods seen between Stratford and West Ham. On a warm day the fireman of ex. GER J15 Class 0-6-0 No 65455 is enjoying the breeze caused by tender-first running. Passenger trains used the pair of lines behind No 65455. (Peter Hay)

54)   A filthy ex. Ministry of Supply Class 8F 2-8-0 No 90246, from 34E New England, waits at the ENGINES MUST STOP board for a path out of 34F Grantham shed and on to the main line in August 1960, prior to taking up a southbound freight working. 90246 remained at New England until October 1963 whence it was drafted to 36E Retford where it ended its days in April 1965. (H. H. Bleads)

55)   Recently outshopped from Stratford Works and with the lined black paintwork glistening in the early Autumn sunshine, ex. GER designed N7/5 0-6-2T No 69635 (depot unknown) waits to be returned to normal duties in the shed yard at 30A Stratford on 16th October 1955. This version of the N7/1 Class had been rebuilt post 1943 with a round-topped firebox. (A. N. H. Glover)

56)   Super power at Kings Cross station in July 1962. A 34A Kings Cross A4 Class 4-6-2 No 60017 *Silver Fox*, in ex. works condition, and 52B Heaton based A3 Class 4-6-2 No 60083 *Sir Hugo* combine to double-head a down Newcastle bound express. *Silver Fox* had been equipped with a double chimney in May 1957. *Sir Hugo* had been similarly equipped in August 1959 followed by the fitting of German smoke deflectors in February 1962. (N. E. Preedy)

57)   Ex. GER J65 Class 0-6-0T No 68211 is at peace with the world on a back road at its home shed of 32B Ipswich on
        30th May 1953. Observe that the coupling rods are only attached to two sets of driving wheels instead of all three. This
        was done to enable the engine to work on the sharp curves in the docks. Built at Stratford Works in 1889, 68211 was
        to be withdrawn in November 1953. (F. Hornby)

58)   The gantries and wires at Clacton herald the forthcoming overhead electric traction, but B1 Class 4-6-0 No 61233, from
        30A Stratford, is still in charge of the 3.55 pm three coach local passenger from Colchester to Clacton on 17th June
        1958. Transferred to 31B March in September 1961, 61233 was withdrawn in November 1963. It then became a
        Departmental engine being numbered 21 and continued on these duties until final withdrawal in April 1966. (Peter Hay)

59)   A trio of railwaymen observe the arrival of A4 Class 4-6-2 No 60006 *Sir Ralph Wedgwood* (34A Kings Cross) as it coasts into Peterborough (North) with an up express bound for London on 6th August 1960. Ousted by diesel power in England, *Sir Ralph Wedgwood* was sent to the Scottish Region in October 1963 where it served at 64A St. Margarets and 61B Ferryhill sheds until withdrawn in September 1965. (F. Hornby)

60)   To provide for the needs of the huge steelworks complex at Scunthorpe a steam shed was situated at Frodingham, coded 36C. Two smoke- blackened visiting ex. GC 04/1 Class 2-8-0's Nos. 63587 (40E Colwick) and 63664 (41J Langwith Junction) await their next duties. Frodingham shed closed in February 1966 being replaced by a modern diesel depot. (H. H. Bleads)

61) One of the magnificently proportioned and handsome British Railways built (1948) A1 Class 4-6-2's No 60120 *Kittiwake*, allocated to 56C Copley Hill, storms homewards through Potters Bar at the head of the 6.10 pm express from Kings Cross to Bradford on 25th July 1956. A section of this lengthy train is also bound for Hull (Paragon). (J. Head)

62) A characteristic feature of the ex. GER shunting engines was the 'hunched-up' look, given by putting the dome behind the chimney and having large, rather slab-sided tanks. In fact J69/1 Class 0-6-0T No 68565 would be just as happy working a London suburban train out of Liverpool Street as standing in the shed yard at 32C Lowestoft on 6th April 1956. (Peter Hay)

63)   Many depots on British Railways had their own lifting facilities to do non-major repair work on their locomotives.
        Ex. GER J17 Class 0-6-0 No 65521 has been hoisted unceremoniously into the air for attention to its driving wheels at
        its home shed of 31C Kings Lynn on 19th September 1953. In the right background is another local engine in the
        shape of ex. GER J69/2 Class 0-6-0T No 68498. (A. N. H. Glover)

64)   Gresley V2 Class 2-6-2 No 60814, from 34A Kings Cross, rattles over points on a through road at Doncaster at the
        head of a lengthy express freight, whilst being observed by a large group of spotters on 23rd April 1959. 60814
        remained at Kings Cross until June 1962 when it was re- allocated to 34F Grantham, but less than twelve months
        later, in April 1963 it was taken out of service. (John Stones)

65)   The fireman of his ex. works charge in the shape of WD Class 8F 2-8-0 No 90270, from 41F Mexborough looks forwards along the boiler as it rattles a mineral train through the ex. Great Central station at Crowle Central en route to Scunthorpe in May 1959. 90270 was later transferred to 34E New England in November 1961 being withdrawn from there in December 1962. (H. H. Bleads)

66)   The immaculate condition of a locally based K1 Class 2-6-0 No 62018 is slightly spoilt by the stains on the cylinder casing whilst at rest in the shed yard at 31B March on 24th April 1955. The status of this former Great Eastern Railway depot was enhanced in later years when it received an allocation of BR *Britannia* Class 4-6-2's. The depot closed to steam towards the end of 1963. (A. N. H. Glover)

67)   Constructed in 1924, A3 Class 4-6-2 No 60068 *Sir Visto* is fresh from overhaul at the 'Plant' and is noted on shed at 36A Doncaster on 12th April 1959. *Sir Visto* is awaiting a suitable duty which will enable it to return to its home shed at 12C Carlisle (Canal). At this stage in time there were three other A3's at Canal, these being Nos 60079 *Bayardo*, 60093 *Coronach* and 60095 *Flamingo*. (A. N. H. Glover)

68)   We take our leave of the Eastern Region with this evocative photograph of L1 Class 2-6-4T No 67746 (34D Hitchin) which is in charge of an engineers breakdown train at LNW Junction, Peterborough in September 1958. The superb girder bridge, carrying the East Coast Main Line over the River Nene, provides a splendid background to this picture. (A. C. Ingram)

CHAPTER TWO – NORTH EASTERN REGION

69) A visitor to the shed at 55E Normanton, a not too clean 56F Low Moor LMS *Jubilee* Class 4-6-0 No 45565 *Victoria* is dwarfed by the huge concrete coaling plant as it simmers in the shed yard on 27th June 1965. At this date in time this was the only LMS named locomotive on the books at Low Moor. Normanton, a shed of Lancashire & Yorkshire origin closed in situ in October 1967. (J. K. Carter)

70)   One of the diminutive ex. L & Y Class 0F 0-4-0 Saddle Tanks, No 51241, in a quite disgraceful condition 'poses' for her picture in Goole freight yard in September 1959. Based at the nearby local shed of 53E, 51241 survived in service there until condemned in January 1962. This close-up shows clearly how cramped the conditions were on the footplate where half of the cab is taken up with its coal supply. (H. H. Bleads)

71)   One of the resident ex. NER J27 Class 0-6-0's No 65796 shares the shed yard at 52E Percy Main with an unidentified sister engine on 4th September 1960. Transferred to 52B Heaton in September 1962, 65796 returned to Percy Main in June 1963. It departed again, this time for good in February 1965, to 52F Blyth where it was to die, in May 1966. (N. L. Browne)

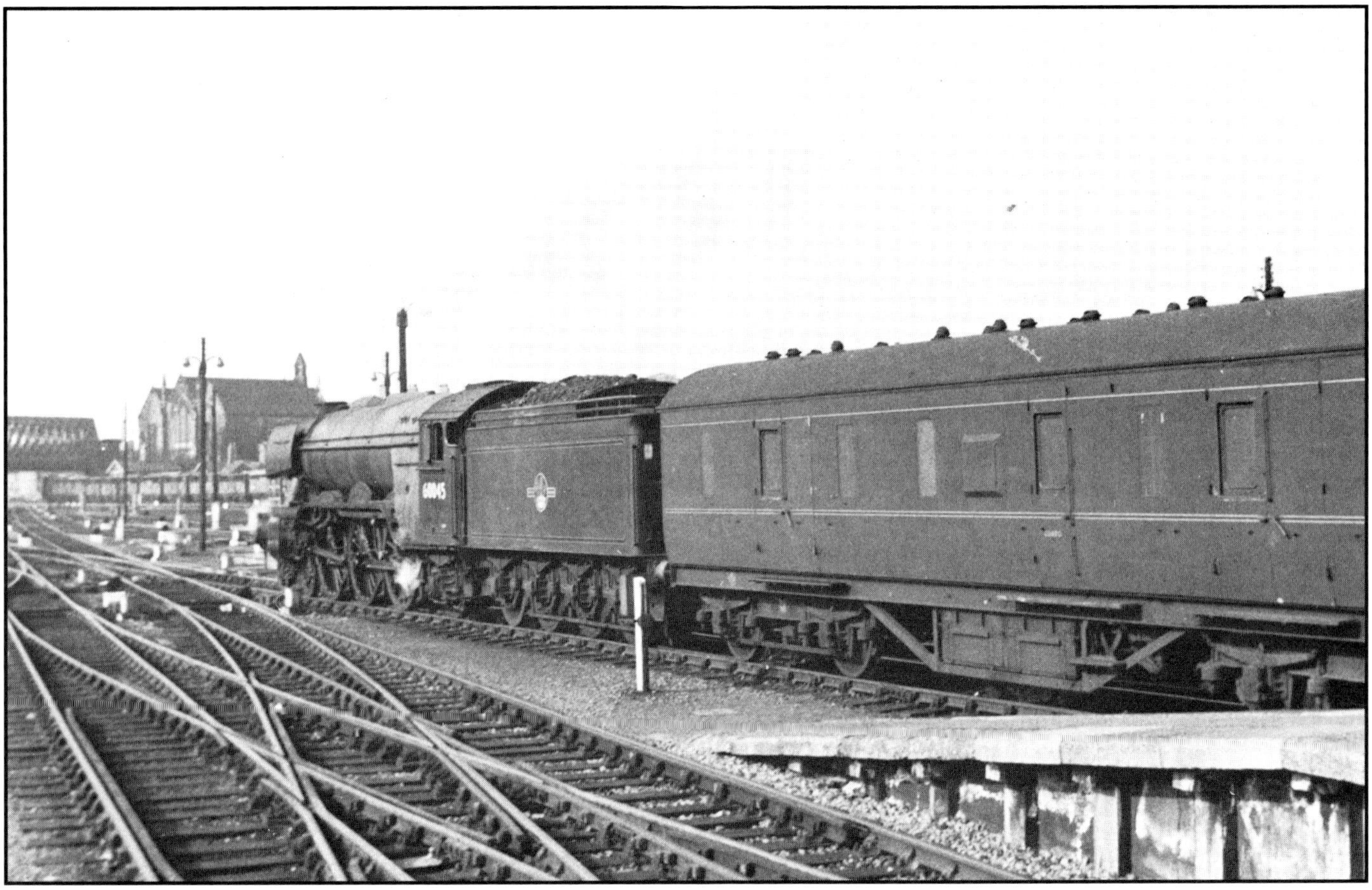

72)   A3 Class 4-6-2 No 60045 *Lemberg* (52A Gateshead) departs from York and prepares to negotiate the complicated
pointwork to the south of the station in May 1962 with an up express. *Lemberg* is in final form with a double chimney,
fitted in October 1959, and with German smoke deflectors with which she was equipped in November 1961.
(H. N. James)

73)   The gloomy interior of the roundhouse at 51C West Hartlepool on 4th September 1960. From left to right are – J72
Class 0-6- 0T No 68707 (withdrawn April 1962), J77 Class 0-6-0T No 68410 (withdrawn October 1960) and J71 Class
0-6-0T No 68233 (withdrawn March 1961). All were of North Eastern Railway design and based at West Hartlepool.
The smoke vents above the locomotives look like giant speakers off very old fashioned record players. (N. L. Browne)

74) The former Great Northern Railway shed at Ardsley had passed from the Eastern to the North Eastern Region in 1956 and was allocated the code 56B. In the shed yard on 14th September 1958 was one of its resident ex. LMS Class 3F 0-6-0 Tanks No 47463. Some members of this class were destined to survive until 1967 but for 47463 withdrawal was on the horizon, in December 1960. (A. N. H. Glover)

75) Newcastle (Central) in its prime was a paradise for train-spotters of all ages. Negotiating the station tender-first on down coal empties on 11th April 1962 is ex. NER Q6 Class 0-8-0 No 63429 from 52C Blaydon. In the background is the famous New Castle to the left of which is the main line to Scotland. To the right of the Castle are the lines which double back over the High Level bridge to Gateshead. (D. Alexander)

76) Engine and Brake to the next port of call was a daily part of any of the goods train links in the North East coalfield for over a century. Ex. NER J27 Class 0-6-0 No 65871 is just coming on to level track at South Pelaw on 13th August 1956. In the distance an iron ore train, banked in the rear, is beginning to climb the 1 in 56 by which this deviation line avoided the rope-worked 1 in 24 Waldridge Bank. (Peter Hay)

77) Ex. North Eastern Railway and later LNER J72 Class 0-6-0T No 68723, a 52A Gateshead engine, is photographed on station pilot duty at Newcastle Central on 28th June 1956. Examples of this class were to continue on this duty until late in 1963. 68723 was itself taken out of service from Gateshead in September 1963 and scrapped at Darlington Works the following month. (J. D. Gomersall)

78)   Eighteen months after nationalisation and the logo of its new owners is printed on the tender of ex. NER J27 Class 0-6-0 No 65800 as it poses for the camera in the yard at 51E Stockton on 12th June 1949. 65800 had a further thirteen years of service in front of it when this picture was taken. It was destined to be withdrawn from 52F Blyth in September 1962. (A. N. H. Glover)

79)   Smoke, steam and a duet of ex. works locomotives prepare to work to their home sheds on 22nd June 1952 in the yard at 51A Darlington after being overhauled at Darlington Plant. On the left is a far from home ex. LMS Class 4 2-6-4T No 42084, from 73A Stewarts Lane on the Southern Region. To the right of 42084 is a 51C West Hartlepool based ex. NER A8 Class 4-6-2T No 69871. (A. N. H. Glover)

80) The sole surviving ex. NER T1 Class 4-8-0 No 69921, in grimy condition, lurks within the gloomy roundhouse at 52H Tyne Dock, its home shed, on 4th September 1960. The other nine surviving members of the class had been withdrawn between March 1957 and November 1959. 69921 lasted until June 1961. Next to 69921 is ex. NER J21 Class 0-6-0 No 65099. (F. Hornby)

81) A4 Class 4-6-2 No 60021 *Wild Swan,* in pristine condition, struggles for adhesion due to the rainswept conditions, as it attempts to depart from York with an up Kings Cross express on 27th June 1959. *Wild Swan,* for many years a 34A Kings Cross locomotive, was transferred to 34E New England upon the closure of the 'Top Shed' in June 1963, along with sister engines from the same depot – Nos 60006/7/8/10/17/25/26/29/32 & 34. (R. W. Hinton)

82)	Swathed in smoke and steam, Peppercorn A2 Class 4-6-2 No 60526 *Sugar Palm* presents a fine sight as it accelerates through Thirsk, between York and Northallerton with an unknown express working – circa 1956. Built by British Railways in 1948, this 50A York based engine only had a working life of fourteen years before being withdrawn in October 1962. (G. W. Sharpe)

83)	In direct contrast to the ancient and gloomy sheds over many parts of the North Eastern Region was 51L Thornaby which became operational in June 1958 with spacious straight sheds, a large roundhouse and workshop. Photographed in the straight running shed on 4th September 1960 is ex. NER Q6 Class 0-8-0 No 63411 which had been transferred from 51D Middlesbrough when Thornaby opened. (N. L. Browne)

84) *The Queen of Scots,* from Kings Cross to Glasgow (Queen Street) via Leeds was officially inaugurated in May 1928 and in October 1960 was still in the capable hands of an elderly Gresley Pacific. 51A Darlington based A3 Class 4-6-2 No 60051 *Blink Bonny* prepares to depart southbound to Leeds with the up express. *Blink Bonny* had already acquired a double chimney (August 1959), to be followed in March 1962 by German deflectors. (N. E. Preedy)

85) Volumes of black smoke pours out of the chimney of A1 Class 4-6-2 No 60126 *Sir Vincent Raven* as it accelerates smartly away from the sharply curved confines of West Hartlepool station with an express in 1960. Regularly a 52B Heaton based engine, *Sir Vincent Raven* moved on to pastures new when drafted to 50A York in August 1961. Named after one of the most famous designers on the North Eastern Railway, 60126 was condemned in January 1965. (N. E. Preedy)

86) A line-up of B1 Class 4-6-0's and BR Class 9F 2-10-0's occupy part of the lengthy shed yard at 50A York on 28th April 1963. Two of the B1's can be identified as Nos 61049, a local engine and 61158, a visitor from 36A Doncaster. 61049 continued in service at York until withdrawn November 1965. 61158 lasted at Doncaster until the end of steam on the Eastern Region, in April 1966. (F. Hornby)

87) A3 Class 4-6-2 No 60071 *Tranquil* (52A Gateshead) drifts into Stockton station in December 1961 with the 1.00 pm cross-country express bound for Colchester. The German smoke deflectors had only been fitted to *Tranquil* the previous month but the double chimney had been fitted three years earlier, in June 1958. 60071 was one of eight A3's cut up by Drapers of Hull between December 1964 and April 1965. (G. D. Appleyard)

88)   52G Sunderland based ex. NER Q6 Class 0-8-0 No 63406 arrives with a train of hopper wagons at Easington Colliery in the East Durham coalfield on 29th May 1964. From January 1957 onwards, 63406 had been allocated to a variety of sheds at Consett, Selby and Tyne Dock before moving to Sunderland in September 1963. It was taken out of service from there in July 1966. (John Stones)

89)   The shed yard at 51A Darlington on an overcast 4th September 1960. In the foreground is Raven ex. NER B16/1 Class 4-6-0 No 61445, a foreigner from 50E Scarborough. Behind 61445 are two unidentified locomotives, a V2 Class 2-6-2 and a WD Class 8F 2-8-0. To the right of 61445 is a WD Class 8F 2-8-0 No 90445, a Darlington engine (N. L. Browne)

90)	There is already an air of dereliction in the surroundings at 52E Percy Main on 18th October 1963. One of the resident ex. NER J27 Class 0-6-0's No 65825 simmers idly in the shed yard. This former North Eastern Railway depot was to close completely in February 1965. Transferred to 52F Blyth upon closure of Percy Main, 65825 only lasted until June 1966. (R. Picton)

91)	Soot stained signal gantries stand sentinel like on each side of A3 Class 4-6-2 No 60056 *Centenary*, from Grantham shed, as it patiently awaits departure from Leeds (Central) station – circa 1957. Fitted with a double chimney in July 1959 and German smoke deflectors in August 1961, *Centenary* was to stay in revenue earning service at 34F Grantham until sentenced to death in May 1963. (M. Joyce)

92)	The vast majority of classes allocated to 55E Normanton were of the ex. LMS or BR Standard varieties including the WD Class 8F 2-8- 0's. There were the odd exceptions and two ex. NER locomotives huddle together in a short siding at the shed on 8th May 1960. Nearest the camera is J72 Class 0-6-0T No 68701 in company with sister engine No 68726. (F. Hornby)

93)	Surrounded by gaunt mills and factories which once upon a time provided handsome rewards for small numbers of people and hard, servile and poorly paid jobs for the remainder, ex. LMS Fowler Class 2-6-4T No 42411, from 56F Low Moor, prepares to leave Sowerby Bridge on excursion duty in March 1964. Sowerby Bridge once had its own shed, coded 56E, which demised in January 1964. (G. W. Sharpe)

94) V2 Class 2-6-2 No 60875, from 36A Doncaster, blasts a haze of grey smoke out of its chimney as it roars through Ripon, between Harrogate and Northallerton, with a heavy express freight in May 1961. Doncaster had quite a number of these fine locomotives on its books over the years, 60875 itself remained there until condemned in March 1962. (G. W. Sharpe)

95) The yard of 53B Hull (Botanic Gardens) plays host to one of its own engines on 31st May 1953 – B1 Class 4-6-0 No 61215 *William Henton Carver,* which has been prepared for a local passenger working. In its hey-day, Hull had three steam sheds, the other two being at Dairycoates and Springhead. Botanic Gardens closed to steam in June 1959. (A. N. H. Glover)

96) Destined to be one of the last steam depots on the North Eastern Region was the former Lancashire & Yorkshire shed at 56F Low Moor. Alongside the shed building in July 1963 is a visitor from 26A Newton Heath in Manchester in the shape of ex. LMS *Jubilee* Class 4-6-0 No 45590 *Travancore*. Low Moor shed closed completely on 1st October 1967. (G. W. Sharpe)

97) Another depot which survived until the end of steam on the North Eastern was at 55D Royston, once owned by the LMS. Lined up in front of the shed building in March 1964 are from left to right – BR Class 9F 2-10-0 No 92110 (16E Kirkby), WD Class 8F 2-8-0 No 90127 and two ex. LMS Class 4F 0-6-0's Nos 43906 and 43968. Royston closed its doors to steam on 6th November 1967. (D. K. Jones)

98) Neatness of stations and around the permanent way was an unusual and pleasing feature of the ex. NER lines of the LNER and BR. Not only is the space between the tracks here at West Hartlepool raked and free of weeds and litter, but small, hardy bushes have been planted. All this stemmed from the work of John Miller, a civil engineer in the 1930's. On the goods avoiding line is ex. NER J27 Class 0-6-0 No 65850 on 11th August 1956. (Peter Hay)

99) It is not often a photograph shows a driver actually driving his engine, but in this view of Newsham in Northumberland, we can see his hand on the regulator through the cab window. The engine under his control is ex. NER J27 Class 0-6-0 No 65810, from 52F Blyth, setting off with a load of coal empties on 15th August 1956. (Peter Hay)

100) A gaggle of spotters relax on one of the platforms and enjoy the warm summer sunshine as the last 'Whitby Willy' or LNER A6 Class 4-6-2T No 69796 performs on station pilot duties at Hull (Paragon) on 29th August 1952. It was withdrawn the following March, having commenced its erstwhile career as a 4-6-0T in 1908. (Peter Hay) 
101) Set in the heart of the dockland was the former Lancashire & Yorkshire freight shed at Goole. This compact depot was over thirty minutes walking time from the nearest station. Captured by the camera on 28th April 1963 are several unidentified locomotives including a BR D67xx Co-Co diesel electric and WD Class 8F 2-8-0 No 90160 a resident of the then coded 50D shed. (F. Hornby)

102) Situated on the East Coast of England is the tidy and popular resort of Scarborough. In steam days it possessed its own depot, coded 50E. It never had a large resident allocation but was to host many 'foreigners' especially during the busy summer months. On 11th May 1961 a visiting B1 Class 4-6-0 No 61030 *Nyala*, from 51A Darlington, leaves the depot for its next duty. (K. Foster)

103) Bright sunshine heralds the arrival of ex. LMS Fowler Class 2-6-4T No 42408, a locally based locomotive, as it arrives at the magnificent station at Huddersfield, passing over the lofty and elegant brick built viaduct on the approaches to the same, with a short express in June 1963. Thanks to its status of being a listed building, Huddersfield station today retains all the grandeur of the old days. (G. W. Sharpe)

104)	A smartly turned out ex. LMS *Jubilee* Class 4-6-0 No 45700 *Amethyst*, a 26A Newton Heath engine, paired with a high-railed Fowler tender, has been coaled and watered and is ready for the road in the shed yard at 55C Farnley Junction on 14th September 1958. Behind *Amethyst* is one of Farnley Junction's own *Jubilee's* No 45581 *Bihar and Orissa*. (A. N. H. Glover)

105)	With its external appearance as filthy as the black smoke pouring from its chimney, 50B Leeds (Neville Hill) A3 Class 4-6-2 No 60036 *Colombo* sets off from Leeds with a *Pullman* express on 5th April 1958. *Colombo* was later equipped with a double chimney in November 1958 and German smoke deflectors in July 1962. The author's are mystified as to what the object is strewn across the tracks in the right foreground? (D. K. Jones)

106) With its tender packed with what appears to be no more than coal slack, WD Class 8F 2-8-0 No 90465, from 51L Thornaby, with steam to spare, ambles along the flat terrain near to Ripon at the head of a Class 8 mineral train on a misty November day in 1958. 90465 was to remain at Thornaby until June 1962 whereupon it was transferred to 56B Ardsley. (G. W. Sharpe)

107) At 51C West Hartlepool there was a small yard between the roundhouse and the straight shed for stabling a few locomotives. Resting between duties on 4th September 1960 is a resident of West Hartlepool, ex. NER Q6 Class 0-8-0 No 63422. This locomotive was withdrawn, being surplus to requirements, from 51C in May 1964 being cut up at Darlington Works two months later. (F. Hornby)

108) This picture typifies the inner city railway industrial scene of yester-year, with steam, semaphore signals, a maze of tracks, a gloomy underpass and factory buildings all on view. A 55A Leeds (Holbeck) ex. LMS *Jubilee* Class 4-6-0 No 45568 *Western Australia* struggles towards the camera with a ten coach local passenger at Leeds on 21st February 1961. (D. K. Jones)

109) V2 Class 2-6-2 No 60927, from 64B Haymarket, is on a running in turn following overhaul at Darlington. It is seen here in the mid-fifties, drawing out of the loop and passing the brick built signalbox at Pilmoor North, between Thirsk and York with a southbound mineral train. 60927 was to remain in Scotland, alternating between Haymarket and St. Margarets (Edinburgh) before being condemned in December 1962. (G. W. Sharpe)

110) As grey as its surroundings, a work-stained ex. NER J27 Class 0-6-0 No 65832, from 52G Sunderland, is at rest in the shed yard at 51A Darlington on 4th September 1960. Constructed in May 1909, 65832 was withdrawn from Sunderland in March 1962 and scrapped at Willoughbys, Choppington in June 1966. Behind 65832 is a diesel shunter in the shape of 0-6-0 No D3139. (F. Hornby)

111) Behind ex. NER J25 Class 0-6-0 No 65727 (52F Blyth) shunting at Newsham station on 15th August 1956 there is a fine array of semaphore signals. On some of the 'dolls', LNER upper quadrant arms have replaced the lower wooden arms supplied to the NER by McKenzie & Holland. The engine's roomy cab with two side windows is typical of late NER locomotive design, by the Worsdell family. (Peter Hay)

112) This picture at Holgate platform York on 30th August 1952 shows the original form of the North Eastern Railway's last 4-6-0 design, the S3, later LNER B16 Class. No 61425 was never rebuilt and still has splashers and a low running plate. Inside Stephenson valve gear is fitted, with a steam reverser and a Darlington pattern cab with low set windows. 61425 was withdrawn from 50A York in September 1961. (Peter Hay)

113) Maximum track occupation outside 55C Farnley Junction shed on 14th September 1958. From left to right are ex. LMS locomotives – *Jubilee* Class 4-6-0 No 45581 *Bihar and Orissa*, a quartet of Class 8F 2-8- 0's Nos 48329 (9F Heaton Mersey), 48473 (55D Royston), 48311 (55B Stourton), 48291 (5B Crewe – South) and Class 5 4-6-0 No 45021 (5A Crewe – North). Most of these locomotives had been involved in excursion duties. (A. N. H. Glover)

114) There must have been a dire shortage of cleaners at 51L Thornaby judging by the horrendous external condition of all these locomotives lined up in the shed yard on 4th September 1960. On view are a selection of J26 & J27 Class 0-6-0's and Q6 Class 0-8-0's. Nearest the camera is Q6 Class 0-8-0 No 63451, a local engine. Thornaby closed its doors to steam in December 1964. (F. Hornby)

115) The peaceful tranquility of the countryside around Monkton Moor is disturbed for a few minutes as J39 Class 0-6-0 No 64706 (50D Starbeck) and A3 Class 4-6-2 No 60074 *Harvester* (50B Leeds – Neville Hill) combine to power a heavy parcels train in the summer of 1957. In common with all of the A3's, *Harvester* was to receive a double chimney, in March 1959 but was never equipped with smoke deflectors. (G. W. Sharpe)

116) The 'premier' passenger steam shed in the North East, at 52A Gateshead, had by 18th September 1962 been reduced to a shadow of its former greatness, with the majority of its remaining allocation of steam and visiting engines being confined to the Pacific Shed. On view on this date were 52B Heaton based A3 Class 4-6-2 No 60051 *Blink Bonny* and A1 Class 4-6-2 No 60147 *North Eastern*, from 50A York. (D. K. Jones)

117) Three coach push and pull trains operated a now extinct local service between Sunderland and South Shields in the 1950's, power being generally provided by a G5 Class 0-4-4T like No 67338 which has the cage and hopper type bunker extension. When photographed near Harton in County Durham on 14th August 1956 its push and pull gear was out of action so running round was necessary at each end of the journey. (Peter Hay)

118) A begrimed ex. Midland Railway Class 2P 4-4-0 No 40538, based at 19B Millhouses, makes a spirited departure from Leeds on 28th August 1957 with an unidentified express working. 40538 was re-allocated to 17A Derby two months later ending its days in September 1962, being cut up almost immediately upon withdrawal at Derby Works. (G. W. Sharpe)

119) One of the huge Raven designed North Eastern Railway, later LNER Q7 Class 0-8-0's No 63469, from 52G Sunderland, waits at 51A Darlington shed to be towed to the nearby workshops for overhaul on 11th June 1960. In common with all fifteen members of the class, 63469 was withdrawn at the end of 1962. Behind 63469 are two ex. NER A8 Class 4-6-2 Tanks awaiting scrapping. (M. S. Stokes)

120) One of 52A Gateshead's allocation of A4 Class 4-6-2's No 60023 *Golden Eagle* departs from Newcastle Central in April 1963 with an express bound for Kings Cross. *Golden Eagle* was transferred to the Scottish Region at 64A St. Margarets (Edinburgh) in November 1963 and was withdrawn from 61B Ferryhill (Aberdeen) in October 1964. It was cut up by the Motherwell Machinery and Scrap Co., Wishaw in March 1965. (N. E. Preedy)

121) Photographed by the turntable in bright sunshine at 51E Stockton on 12th June 1949 is B1 Class 4-6-0 No E1290, later 61290. Stockton shed closed completely on 14th June 1959. During the latter years of its life 61290 was based at 68E (later 12C) Carlisle (Canal) from where it was taken out of service in March 1962. Four months later it was reduced to scrap at Cowlairs Works. (A. N. H. Glover)

122) A rebuilt ex. LMS *Patriot* 4-6-0 graces the yard at 55A Leeds (Holbeck) in October 1963. No 45527 *Southport*, from 12A Carlisle (Kingmoor), in fine external condition has just been serviced in readiness to work an excursion. Holbeck, originally a Midland Railway depot, had been in the hands of the North Eastern Region since early 1957. It closed to steam in October 1967. (G. W. Sharpe)

123) Another photograph taken at Holgate station York on 30th August 1952. The locomotive is B16/2 Class 4-6-0 No 61457 which was a Gresley rebuild with Walschaerts valve gear and a high running plate which eliminated the splashers. 61457 is awaiting admission to the goods lines which by-pass York station on its western side, there being more trains on the other side of the platform waiting their turn to go forward. (Peter Hay)

124) Headingley station on the outskirts of Leeds is the setting for this photograph of BR Class 4 2-6-4T No 80120, based at 50B Leeds (Neville Hill), as it approaches with a Leeds to Newcastle express on 8th August 1959. At this stage in time Neville Hill had five of these locomotives on its books Nos 80116-20. All five engines were transferred to the Scottish Region in October 1963. (M. Joyce)

125) One of the few surviving ex. LMS *Jubilee* Class 4-6-0's No 45593 *Kolhapur* (55A Leeds – Holbeck) is photographed outside 56F Low Moor shed on 9th April 1967, the occasion of a visit by the Manchester Locomotive Society. *Kolhapur* was withdrawn from service from Holbeck when the shed closed to steam in October 1967 and is now preserved at Tyseley. (W. Potter)

126) A smoke-blackened A3 Class 4-6-2 No 60056 *Centenary*, from 34F Grantham, is a stranger in the camp as it simmers by the turntable in 50A York's shed yard on 11th April 1960. Built at Doncaster Works in 1925 as an A1 Class its original number was 2555. Later rebuilt as an A3 and renumbered 56, *Centenary* was condemned at Grantham in May 1963 and scrapped at Doncaster six months later. (B. W. L. Brooksbank)

127) The final photograph in the sequence of prints appertaining to the North Eastern Region is taken at Arthington Junction, between Harrogate and Leeds in June 1957. Two War Department Austerity Class 8F 2- 8-0's Nos 90457 (50D Starbeck) and 90076 (51B Newport) double-head a heavy loose-coupled freight train past the camera. Examples of these locomotives were to be seen in great numbers all over the North East until 1967. (G. W. Sharpe)

128) Fife-shire had a plethora of sheds both large and small in steam days, the main ones being at Dundee, Dunfermline and at Thornton Junction. Ex North British J37 Class 0-6-0 No 64547 gurgles and steams gently over an ash pit inside the running shed at its home depot of Dundee Tay Bridge, coded 62B, on 16th July 1966. By this time the end was on the horizon for steam in Scotland with Tay Bridge being one of the last to go in May 1967. 64547 was condemned at Tay Bridge in December 1966 and disposed of by McWilliams, Shettleston in April 1967. (C. P. Stacey)

129) A Great North of Scotland Railway scene at Aberlour, with only the numberplate on the engine and the modern wagons on the right to tell us this is August 1953 and not forty years earlier. Even the carriage is ex. GNSR. D40 Class 4-4-0 No 62269 heads the Speyside goods, shunted here to pass the morning passenger train. Aberlour station closed in 1965. (Peter Hay)

130) A locally based former North British Railway N15 Class 0-6- 2T No 69198 shunts wagons at 65C Parkhead shed in May 1959. Glasgow had a host of steam sheds at one time of which Parkhead was once owned by the North British Railway. It closed as a parent depot in January 1963 becoming a sub-shed of Eastfield. It closed completely on 18th October 1965. (N. E. Preedy)

131) Allocated to 62C Dunfermline, Ex. NBR Y9 Class 0-4-0ST No 68101 was the only member of the class with the vacuum brake, because it had carriage shunting duties. However, on 22nd April 1957, in company with the customary 'coal-cart' or tender, it was shunting in the goods yard of its home station. Note the typical wooden dumb buffers fitted, despite its passenger shunting work. (Peter Hay)

132) In a filthy condition, ex. NBR J88 Class 0-6-0T No 68353 exudes a small amount of sulphur out of its tall and narrow chimney as it rests alongside its home shed building at 62A Thornton Junction in January 1957. Taken out of service from Thornton in February 1962, its last destination was to Arnott Young's scrapyard at Old Kilpatrick where it was cut up in September 1963. (N. E. Preedy)

133) 64A St. Margarets (Edinburgh) had a number of sub-sheds including this one at South Leith, Edinburgh, which consisted of an ash-pit and an office. 'On shed' on 15th May 1954 are two tank engines of North Eastern and North British origins. Nearest the camera is ex. NER J72 Class 0-6-0T No 69014 and behind this engine is ex. NBR Y9 Class 0-4-0ST No 68122. (F. Hornby)

134) Exiled to the former Great North of Scotland Section, ex. GER B12 Class 4-6-0 No 61502 (61A Kittybrewster) was built in 1912 at the Stratford Works of the Great Eastern Railway Company. On 4th August 1953 it was at Keith Junction ready to leave with the 12.25 pm local working to Aberdeen. (Peter Hay)

135) The scene in the shed yard at 61A Kittybrewster (Aberdeen) was full of interest on 5th August 1953. On the left we can see half of the resident snowplough, laid up for the summer. Next comes ex. GNSR D40 Class 4-4-0 No 62260 built in 1889. Behind it is a glimpse of Kittybrewster's 'heavy lifters', the steam breakdown crane. Was it used to lift B1 Class 4-6-0 No 61345, which seems to have wheel problems? (Peter Hay)

136) Filth and grime are all too present in the shed yard at 64A St. Margarets (Edinburgh) on 12th June 1962. A trio of work-stained locomotives await their next duties, from left to right: A3 Class 4-6-2 No 60087 *Blenheim*, A2/3 Class 4-6-2 No 60519 *Honeyway* and ex. NBR J36 Class 0-6-0 No 65327. All three were residents of St. Margarets. (F. Hornby)

137) As can be seen in the extreme right of this picture, the diesel multiple units had arrived in Fife by the 16th September 1961. Ex. North British Railways J37 Class 0-6-0 No 64549, from 62A Thornton Junction, pulls away from its home base towards Cowdenbeath with a short goods train. 64549 remained at Thornton Junction until withdrawn in July 1964. (Peter Hay)

138) Inverbervie station, the terminus of the North British Railway branch line from Montrose had closed in 1951. On 16th June 1960 the weed overgown and rusting tracks hosted an SLS/RCTS special which is being hauled by a specially turned out ex. NBR J37 Class 0-6-0 No 64615 from 62B Dundee Tay Bridge. 64615 is carrying an SLS/RCTS board inscribed with the words 'Scottish Railtours 1960'. (F. Hornby)

139) Awaiting its next working which will perhaps take it on a journey across the Forth and Tay bridges to its home shed at 62B Dundee Tay Bridge, B1 Class 4-6-0 No 61292 basks in bright sunshine on a back road at 64B Haymarket – circa 1957. Withdrawn from Tay Bridge shed in September 1965 the end of the road for 61292 was at Shipbreaking Industries, Faslane in January 1966. (N. E. Preedy)

140) Ex. NBR N15 Class 0-6-2T No 69128 was sent from Thornton Junction to Ferryhill (Aberdeen) in 1932 and it was still allocated there twenty years later when it was photographed on No 2 pilot (note the headcode disc) at Aberdeen Joint station on 3rd September 1952. It carries the traditional wooden footboard below the bunker, with a handrail for the shunter to hang on by as he rode his perch. (Peter Hay)

141) The 3.50 pm Dunfermline (Upper) to Inverkeithing followed a circuitous route via Touch Junction and Dunfermline (Lower) station. At the latter ex. NBR D34 Class 4-4-0 No 62478 *Glen Quoich* (62A Thornton Junction) was passed by B1 Class 4-6-0 No 61072 (62C Dunfermline) heading north on 28th March 1959. Dunfermline (Upper) closed in 1968. (Peter Hay)

142) The footplate crew of a visiting ex. NER J72 Class 0-6-0T No 68733 (65A Eastfield – Glasgow) look towards the camera in the yard at 65C Parkhead on 27th August 1957. During the 1960's there were a number of depots in Scotland which stored redundant steam locomotives prior to scrapping. Parkhead was one such depot. On 23rd November 1963 it held twelve such engines including three ex. LMS *Royal Scot* 4-6-0's and A3 Class 4-6-2 No 60096 *Papyrus*. (N. L. Browne)

143) Standing over a pile of discarded ash, Gresley D49/1 Class 4-4-0 No 62711 *Dumbartonshire* hugs the shed wall within the narrow confines of the yard at 64A St. Margarets (Edinburgh) on 12th June 1960. Note the ex. Great Central Railway tender to which *Dumbartonshire* is paired with. Withdrawn from St. Margarets in May 1961 it was dismantled by its makers at Darlington Works in June 1961. (F. Hornby)

144) Another Great Eastern locomotive far from home. In the 1930's transfer to the GNS section of B12 Class 4-6-0's not rebuilt with large boilers began and some, like No 61507 were actually given new, small, round topped boilers whilst in Scotland. On 3rd September 1952 it is seen leaving Aberdeen with the 3.18 pm to Ballater. On the left is an ex. LMS Class 5 4-6-0 No 45106 at the head of the up West Coast Postal, due away at 3.30 pm. (Peter Hay)

145) Despite a tender full of slack Thompson B1 Class 4-6-0 No 61407 has steam to spare on 5th July 1965. The escaping
      steam disturbs the overhanging branches from the Princes Street Gardens as 61407, a 62C Dunfermline locomotive,
      glides into Edinburgh (Waverley) at the head of a four coach local from Perth. By 1965, steam hauled passenger trains
      at Waverley were becoming a rarity. (N. E. Preedy)

146) Huge chimney stacks from a factory complex dominate the skyline at 65E Kipps, in Glasgow on 27th August 1957.
      Clumps of weeds push their way out of the ground in the shed yard in front of a resident ex. NBR N15 Class 0-6-2T
      No 69206 which is on shunting duties. 69206 remained at Kipps until condemned in May 1960 and it was cut up at
      Cowlairs Works a month later. (N. L. Browne)

147)   Another sub-shed which came under the control of 64A St. Margarets (Edinburgh) was at Seafield, near to the docks. If on foot, it took some sixty minutes to get to it if setting off from Waverley station. Outside the two road structure on 15th May 1954 is an ex. NBR J37 Class 0- 6-0 No 64543. Seafield closed in October 1962. (F. Hornby)

148)   Another shot of ex. NBR J37 Class 0-6-0 No 64543, this time on 16th June 1958. With a mixture of upper and lower quadrants in the background and the crew posing for the camera, 64543 is in charge of a short Class 8 goods train at Dunfermline (Lower) station. Note the sharp dog-leg curve to the right of the train. Withdrawn from 62C Dunfermline in December 1962, 64543 was finally disposed of at Inverurie Works in May 1963. (F. Hornby)

149) A burned and rusted lower portion of its smokebox door suggests that ex. NBR D34 Class 4-4-0 No 62470 *Glen Roy* has had some hard pounding lately, but on 8th August 1953 it was merely running easily down the 1 in 42 from Cowlairs into Glasgow (Queen Street) with a five coach local passenger consisting of some rather decrepit stock. (Peter Hay)

150) A side road at 62A Thornton Junction is the setting for this photograph of ex. NBR N15 Class 0-6-2T No 69132, a local engine, which is swathed in bright sunshine on 21st June 1959. In December of the same year, 69132 was transferred to 66B Motherwell where it eked out the last few months of its existence before being withdrawn in November 1960. It was scrapped at Cowlairs Works in January 1961. (A. N. H. Glover)

151) B1 Class 4-6-0 No 61172 (62B Dundee Tay Bridge) passes the spartan station at Carnoustie with a down mixed freight on 8th June 1965. Carnoustie, situated between Arbroath and Dundee was once the property of the Dundee and Arbroath Joint Railway which was later seconded to both the Caledonian and North British Railways. (K. L. Seal)

152) The Arrochar Motor setting off along the West Highland line at Craigendoran (Upper) station, catching the evening sun on 31st August 1958. As, for so many years, the engine is an ex. NBR C15 Class 4-4-2T, in this instance No 67460, from 65A Eastfield (Glasgow). Craigendoran (Lower) station on the Helensburgh line is on the left. (Peter Hay)

153) A fine view of the turntable and part of the half- roundhouse on a gloomy 21st May 1954, at the former Great North of Scotland shed at 61A Kittybrewster (Aberdeen). With steam issuing from many parts of the locomotive, a filthy dirty ex. NBR D34 Class 4-4-0 No 62493 *Glen Gloy* stands on the turntable. Peeping out of the shed is an unidentified B1 Class 4-6-0. (F. Hornby)

154) With mountainous terrain as a background, an especially cleaned Gresley K4 Class 2-6-0 No 61995 *Cameron of Lochiel,* from 62A Thornton Junction, is being rotated on the turntable at 63B Fort William in the West Highlands on 18th June 1960. *Cameron of Lochiel* was involved on S.L.S. duty on this particular day. In the left of the picture is a B1 Class 4-6-0 No 61307 (64A St. Margarets – Edinburgh). (F. Hornby)

155) Another view of 65C Parkhead, taken in ths shed yard, this time on 15th June 1958. In the foreground is ex. NBR C16 Class 4-4-2T No 67500. Behind 67500 is a Gresley V3 Class 4MT 2-6-2T No 67612, both locomotives being natives of Parkhead. Again, both engines ended their days here, with 67500 being withdrawn in October 1959 and 67612 in January 1961. (F. Hornby)

156) Before the Blue Trains came, the Gresley V1 & V3 Classes of 2-6-2 Tanks worked the heavy suburban and residential traffic on the ex. LNER lines around Glasgow. A typical service was that between Hyndland and Airdrie and on 30th April 1960, No 67605, based at 65E Kipps, was on such a duty, approaching Coatbridge (Sunnyside). As can be seen by the masts, progress on the forthcoming electrification is well under way. (Peter Hay)

157) V2 Class 2-6-2 No 60920 emerges from the 124 yards long Mound Tunnel and coasts into Edinburgh (Waverley) with a stopping train from Aberdeen in the summer of 1957. Being based at 62B Dundee Tay Bridge, 60920 may well have taken over this train at Dundee. Above the Mound Tunnel is Scotland's National Gallery and in the far distance is the 1009 yards long Haymarket South Tunnel. (N. E. Preedy)

158) Another former North British shed was at Bathgate, coded 64F, situated roughly half-way between Edinburgh and Glasgow. In steam in the shed yard in September 1954 are two resident ex. NBR 4-4-0's — D34 Class No 62495 *Glen Luss* and D30 Class No 62439 *Father Ambrose*. Bathgate once boasted two stations, an Upper and a Lower. Bathgate (Lower) closed in 1930 and Bathgate (Upper) in 1956. (L. Brownhill)

159) Its paintwork gleaming after overhaul at Cowlairs Works, ex. NBR C16 Class 4-4-2T No 67484 waits in the yard at 65A Eastfield (Glasgow) to be returned to its home shed at 62B Dundee Tay Bridge in October 1957. This may well have been the last occasion that 67484 was to undergo major repairs as it was withdrawn from Tay Bridge shed in April 1960. (N. E. Preedy)

160) Electrification work, which will spell the end for steam on these services in this part of Glasgow was well under way at Partick Hill Junction to the west of the city in 1960. Prior to the demise of steam, a smoke-blackened Gresley V1 Class 2-6-2T No 67655, from 65C Parkhead, works a typical suburban train formed of BR and LNER carriages. (Peter Hay)

161) The pioneer 'Glen' or ex. NBR D34 Class 4-4-0 No 62467 *Glenfinnan* arrives at Thornton Junction with the 12.48 pm local passenger from Crail on the Fife Coast. A horsebox brings up the rear of this four coach train on 22nd April 1957. *Glenfinnan*, a 62A Thornton Junction engine was withdrawn from there in August 1960 and cut up at Cowlairs Works three months later. (Peter Hay)

162) A partially demolished building overlooks the yard at 65E Kipps shed on 15th June 1958. In the foreground is one of the diminutive ex. NBR Y9 Class 0-4-0 Saddle Tanks No 68100. In the left background is sister engine No 68108 and like 68100 was a resident of Kipps shed. The depot closed to steam in January 1963 but was used for storage purposes for some time afterwards. (F. Hornby)

163) One of the very distinctive ex. GNSR Z4 Class 0-4-2 Tanks No 68190 was based at 61A Kittybrewster, where it was photographed on 5th August 1953. Built by Manning, Wardle & Co., in 1915, its appearance suggests that it was improvised out of an 0-6-0T design, but its railway owners never altered it in any detail and it looked a typical product of its makers until scrapped in 1960. (Peter Hay)

164) A3 Class 4-6-2 No 60057 *Ormonde* (64B Haymarket) passes Princes Street Gardens on its way into Edinburgh (Waverley) with a mixed parcels and passenger train in August 1961. The locomotive was soon to enter Doncaster Works for its last overhaul and for the fitting of German smoke deflectors. *Ormonde*, equipped with a double chimney in October 1958, was named after the winner of the Derby, 2,000 guineas and St. Ledger races in 1886. (N. E. Preedy)

165) One of the superheated 4-4-0's of LNER D40 Class, No 62277 *Gordon Highlander* is now preserved at Glasgow Transport Museum. On 6th August 1953 it was working the Speyside branch from Boat of Garten and here it stands at Craigellachie with a mid-morning train. The second carriage is a former GNSR corridor composite, with swing, rather than sliding doors between the corridor and the compartments. (Peter Hay)

166) Steamed and ready for the road, K4 Class 2-6-0 No 61996 *Lord of the Isles* displays its handsome lines in the busy yard at 62A Thornton Junction on 16th June 1958. In common with the other K4's *Lord of the Isles* was allocated to 65A Eastfield (Glasgow) at this stage in time. All of them were transferred to Thornton Junction in December 1959. Built at Darlington in December 1938 it was withdrawn in October 1961. (F. Hornby)

167) In the distance, the Edinburgh & Glasgow main line signals are 'off' for an express, as an ex. NBR J37 Class 0-6-0 No 64547 plods along towards Edinburgh with a loose-coupled goods train from Fife via the Forth Bridge in 1957. 64547, from 64A St. Margarets, still retains its lock up safety valves and was destined to be one of the last working members of this, the final NBR goods design, being withdrawn in December 1966. (Peter Hay)

168) Eighteen months into nationalisation and the logo of London North Eastern is still displayed on the tender of ex. NBR D29 Class 4-4-0 No 62402 *Redgauntlet*, seen here awaiting attention at Cowlairs Works on 5th June 1949. At nationalisation in January 1948 there were ten survivors of this 1909 built class. (A. N. H. Glover)

169) Another 1949 photograph, this time taken on 8th June at 62B Dundee Tay Bridge. The stencilled lettering of BRITISH RAILWAYS can just be seen through the grime on the tender of V2 Class 2-6-2 No 60882. This locomotive is still without a BR style front numberplate. Behind 60882 is an unidentified War Department Class 8F 2-8-0. (A. N. H. Glover)

170) Steam drifts gently from the safety valves of A3 Class 4-6-2 No 60043 *Brown Jack*, equipped with a double chimney in February 1959, as this 64B Haymarket engine draws the empty stock of an excursion into Edinburgh (Waverley) station in 1960. Fitted with German smoke deflectors in February 1962, *Brown Jack* was withdrawn from 64A St. Margarets in May 1964, stored at 64F Bathgate and then cut up by Motherwell Machinery & Scrap Co., Wishaw in August 1964. (N. E. Preedy)

171) Another view of Edinburgh (Waverley), this time taken on 9th April 1957. It is of the showpiece pilot at the west end of the station, ex. NBR J83 Class 0-6-0T No 68481, the pride of 64B Haymarket. The special touches include painted borders to the front number and shedplates. 68481 survived in service at Haymarket until condemned in February 1962. (Peter Hay)

172) An ex. LMS influence on the former Great North of Scotland Railway at Elgin on 18th June 1958 in the shape of Class 2P 4-4-0 No 40618, allocated to 61C Keith. 40618 is presumably waiting to take over a local passenger working if the headcode displayed on the smokebox door is correct. Transferred to 61B Ferryhill in July 1961, 40618 was withdrawn two months later and cut up at Inverurie Works in November 1961. (N. L. Browne)

173) Originally of Gresley Great Northern design, a number of J50/3 0-6-0 Tanks were based at depots in Scotland. In May 1959 one of the stud of these locomotives allocated to 65A Eastfield (Glasgow) No 68955 simmers gently in the yard of its home shed. All of these engines allocated to Eastfield were gone by September 1960, 68955 itself being withdrawn in December 1959. (N. E. Preedy)

174) Seen in steam in the shed yard at 62C Dunfermline on 16th June 1958 is one of the resident Gresley V3 Class 2-6-2's No 67672. Built at Doncaster Works in November 1938 as a V1 Class engine, 67672 has straight steampipes and a modified coal bunker. Withdrawn from Dunfermline in December 1962 it was not cut up until twelve months later by Campbells of Airdrie. (F. Hornby)

175)	A virtually brand new BR Class 4 2-6-4T No 80107 shows off its compact and powerful lines in the yard near to the turntable at 61A Kittybrewster on 26th June 1956. 80107 was re-allocated to 66A Polmadie (Glasgow) in April 1957 and was destined to end its brief working days at this shed in September 1964. Kittybrewster closed to steam in the summer of 1961. (A. N. H. Glover)

176)	Keith Junction, of Great North of Scotland Railway origin, is the focus of interest for the photographer on 14th June 1960. Busy shunting in the goods yard is a very unkempt looking ex. NBR J36 Class 0-6-0 No 65277 based at the nearby shed. Also shunting in the yard to the left of 65277 is a Barclay manufactured 0-4-0 diesel shunter No D2417. (F. Hornby)

177)   This stores van was a relic of bygone times when photographed at Edinburgh (Waverley) in September 1952. A Great
North of Scotland Railway six-wheeler dating from the turn of the century, it spent a humble existence carrying stores
and spare parts between Cowlairs Works in Glasgow and outlying motive power depots. (Peter Hay)

178)   Looking in fine external fettle on 16th June 1958 is an ex. NBR 'Scott' D30 Class 4-4-0 No 62431 *Kenilworth,* in steam
in the yard of its home shed at 62A Thornton Junction. *Kenilworth* was constructed in October 1914 and withdrawn
from Thornton in November 1958. Next to *Kenilworth,* in equally clean condition, is ex. NBR J37 Class 0-6-0 No
64635 another local engine. (F. Hornby)

179) Bathed in warm Spring sunshine is another ex. NBR 'Scott' D30 Class 4-4-0 No 62427 *Dumbiedykes* seen here in the shed yard at 62C Dunfermline, to which it belonged, on 16th May 1954. Withdrawn from Dunfermline in April 1959 it was eventually scrapped at Inverurie Works in September 1959. Next to *Dumbiedykes* is a 'Rider & Tool' van No E971513. (F. Hornby)

180) A 62B Dundee Tay Bridge based A2 Class 4-6-2 No 60528 *Tudor Minstrel* storms under several signal gantries as it passes one of the signalboxes at Haymarket with a down Dundee express in September 1957. After spells at 63A Perth and 61B Ferryhill between May 1960 and June 1961, *Tudor Minstrel* returned to Tay Bridge. It remained there until April 1966 when once again it was drafted to Ferryhill being taken out of service from there in June 1966. (R. W. Hinton)

181) A Tay-side suburban train beside the river at West Ferry on the Dundee and Arbroath Joint line between Dundee and Broughty Ferry on 5th April 1958. Ex. NBR C16 Class 4-4-2T No 67502, from Tay Bridge shed, is hauling, bunker-first, the 12.41 pm Dundee to Arbroath local passenger train. The six coaches are all LMS of the 1925 variety. (Peter Hay)

182) 64A St. Margarets (Edinburgh) was a shed of two parts. The main running shed was next to the down main line and opposite was an uncovered roundhouse. Gathered round the turntable in various pre- nationalisation liveries in June 1948 are three tank engines. From left to right are: Y9 Class 0-4-0ST No 68097 and J83 Class 0-6-0 Tanks Nos 68450 and 68474, All three are of North British Railway origin. (G. W. Sharpe)

183) A final glimpse of the shed scene at 65E Kipps, taken on 15th June 1958. From left to right are: ex. NER J72 Class 0-6-0T No 68733 and two ex. NBR Y9 Class 0-4-0 Saddle Tanks Nos 68110 and 68100. To the modern railway enthusiasts of the 1980's the use of the 'coal carts' as attached to the 0-4-0 Saddle Tanks must be laughable, but they served their purpose. Kipps shed was a five minute walk from Coatbridge Sunnyside station. (N. L. Browne)

184) The East Coast Main Line ran over the Dundee & Arbroath Joint line north-east from Dundee and carried something of a suburban service as far as Arbroath. This is the 3.43 pm from Arbroath waiting to leave for Dundee (East) on 5th April 1958. The engine is an ex. NBR C16 Class 4-4-2T No 67486, based at 62B Dundee Tay Bridge as the buffer beam inscription tells us. Dundee (East) station closed the following January. (Peter Hay)